MINIATURE HORSES

By Barbara M. Linde

Gareth Stevens
Publishing

Please visit our Web site, www.garethstevens.com. For a free color catalog of all our high-quality books, call toll free 1-800-542-2595 or fax 1-877-542-2596.

Library of Congress Cataloging-in-Publication Data

Linde, Barbara M.
 Miniature horses / Barbara M. Linde.
     p. cm. – (Horsing around)
 Includes index.
 ISBN 978-1-4339-4632-5 (pbk.)
 ISBN 978-1-4339-4633-2 (6-pack)
 ISBN 978-1-4339-4631-8 (library binding)
 1. Miniature horses–Juvenile literature. I. Title.
 SF293.M56L56 2011
 636.1'09–dc22

                                   2010029689

First Edition

Published in 2011 by
Gareth Stevens Publishing
111 East 14th Street, Suite 349
New York, NY 10003

Copyright © 2011 Gareth Stevens Publishing

Designer: Michael J. Flynn
Editor: Therese Shea

Photo credits: Cover, p. 1, (cover, back cover, p. 1 wooden sign), (front cover, pp. 2–4, 7–8, 10, 13–14, 17–18, 20–24 wood background), back cover (wood background), pp. 5, 11–13 Shutterstock.com; p. 6 Ed Clark/Time & Life Pictures/Getty Images; p. 9 G. Adams/ Hulton Archive/Getty Images; p. 15 Eri Morita/Riser/Getty Images; pp. 16–17 Haiku Expressed/First Light/Getty Images; p. 19 Robyn Beck/AFP/Getty Images; p. 20 Spencer Platt/Getty Images.

Printed in the United States of America

CPSIA compliance information: Batch #CW11GS: For further information contact Gareth Stevens, New York, New York at 1-800-542-2595.

Contents

What Is a Miniature Horse?. 4

How Small! 7

Pets and Workers. 8

Where They Live 10

What They Eat 13

Staying Healthy 14

Grooming 17

Good Pets 18

Guide Horses. 20

Glossary 22

For More Information. 23

Index 24

Words in the glossary appear in **bold** type the first time they are used in the text.

The word "**miniature**" means a smaller form of something. Do you collect miniature cars? They look like real cars, but they're much smaller. Have you seen a miniature rose? It looks, smells, and grows like a regular rose, but it's a smaller size.

A miniature horse is a special **breed** of horse. It's NOT a pony. It's NOT a donkey. You might even think a miniature horse is a baby horse, but it's not. It's a horse, but much smaller! Only size makes a miniature horse different from any other horse breed.

Like other horses, miniature horses like to run and play.

THE MANE FACT

Ponies and horses are different. Ponies usually have thicker necks, wider bodies, and shorter legs.

A baby miniature horse weighs about 20 pounds (9 kg) and is about 20 inches (51 cm) tall. Some are much smaller.

The miniature horse breed has come from small horses having families for centuries. Finally, they reached the size they are today. A miniature horse is no more than 34 inches (86 cm) tall, from its foot to its shoulder. A regular-size horse may be as much as 72 inches (183 cm) from foot to shoulder. A miniature horse usually weighs about 200 pounds (90 kg). A regular-size horse can weigh up to 2,200 pounds (1,000 kg). That's a big difference!

In the 1600s, miniature horses were popular in Europe as pets for royalty. Some were used in circuses. Later, miniature horses were put to work in underground mines in Great Britain. They were small enough to fit through narrow tunnels, where other horses couldn't fit.

In the late 1800s, people brought miniature horses from Great Britain to the United States. When machines took over work in the mines, miniature horses weren't needed. Now most miniature horses are pets. Some people race their miniature horses. Others display them in shows.

Three children ride miniature horses around a track in England in 1926.

THE MANE FACT

The first miniature horse came to the United States in 1888.

A miniature horse can live for about 35 years. It n

good care. Although a miniature horse can stay ir

for hours, it likes the outdoors best. A sunny r

of its favorite places. It can rest and run ·

miniature horse also needs a place

and rain, such as a small barn

A miniature horse shc·

large horse might kick

harm the small a·

Miniature horses rarely sit.
They like to lay down or stand.

THE MANE FACT

A miniature horse named Angel lived
more than 50 years!

11

Like other horses, miniature horses can be many colors.

What They Eat

Miniature horses are small, but they can eat a lot. They eat grass, hay, and grains. They also need salt. Sometimes their owners set out bricks of salt for them to lick. Miniature horses also need lots of cool, clean water to drink.

Miniature horses may eat too much. Many owners try to prevent this by giving their horses two small meals each day. They don't let the horses stay in the pasture eating grass for too long.

THE MANE FACT

Miniature horses like sweets, such as apples, candy, and soda! Too many sweets are not healthy for them.

To stay healthy, miniature horses need regular **medical** care. Most owners work with a **veterinarian**. The horse gets shots to prevent illnesses. Miniature horses also need to have their teeth cleaned.

Miniature horses need care for their hoofs. They don't wear horseshoes, so their hoofs have to be cleaned every day. About every 6 to 8 weeks, they should have their hoofs **trimmed**. This is done by a person with special training called a farrier.

THE MANE FACT

A miniature horse can't carry more than 70 pounds (32 kg).

Children can ride miniature horses, but adults can't.

15

THE MANE FACT

Miniature horses grow a thicker
coat for the winter months.
They **shed** this hair in spring.

16

Grooming

It's important to **groom** a miniature horse every day. A special brush and comb are used on the horse's hair. Brushing and combing make the mane and tail smooth. Brushing also picks out bugs. The horse's hair looks clean and shiny after it is brushed. If necessary, a little fly spray on the horse's coat helps keep pests away.

A miniature horse doesn't need baths often. The horse's coat has natural oils that keep it healthy. Too much water will take away the oils.

Miniature horses are usually very gentle, which makes them good pets.

Most people keep miniature horses as pets. Miniature horses enjoy being around people. Like dogs, miniature horses can learn to obey a person's orders. Some horses know how to tap a hoof on a door when they need to go outside! Miniature horses also make good visitors for sick or **elderly** people.

Owners may enter their miniature horses in shows and **competitions**. Others raise them to sell. There are several clubs for miniature horses and their owners.

Though miniature horses can't carry adults, they're strong enough to pull people in carts.

THE MANE FACT

Just like regular horses, a boy miniature horse is called a stallion. A girl is called a mare.

Guide Horses

A miniature horse's eyes are far back on its head, so it can see almost all the way behind itself without turning. It can see in dark places, too. Because of these features, miniature horses can be guides for people who are blind.

Guide horses go through special training to learn to help their owners walk on streets, go shopping, and get around their homes. Sometimes the horses go on buses or airplanes. A guide horse named Dervish learned to pull on a blanket and turn the light off before going to sleep!

Thumbelina, the world's smallest horse

The World's Smallest Horse*

Name	Thumbelina
Birth Date	May 1, 2001
Home	Goose Creek Farm in St. Louis, Missouri
Weight at Birth	8.5 pounds (3.9 kg)
Weight Now	60 pounds (27 kg)
Height at Birth	11 inches (28 cm)
Height Now	17.5 inches (44.5 cm)

*In 2010, a miniature horse named Einstein was born weighing 6 pounds (2.7 kg). He stood about 14 inches (36 cm) tall. Guinness World Records will compare Einstein to Thumbelina when he's 4.

21

Glossary

breed: a group of animals that share features different from others of that kind

competition: an activity in which people try to do something better than others

elderly: past middle age

groom: to clean and look after an animal

medical: having to do with care given by doctors

miniature: a smaller form of something

pasture: grass-covered land where animals eat

shed: to lose

trim: to clip or cut down in size

veterinarian: a doctor who is trained to treat animals

For More Information

Books:

Hansen, Rosanna. *Panda: A Guide Horse for Ann*. Honesdale, PA: Boyds Mill Press, 2005.

Lunis, Natalie. *Miniature Horses*. New York, NY: Bearport Publishing, 2010.

Robb, Johnny, and Jan Westmark. *The Big Book of Small Equines: A Celebration of Miniature Horses and Shetland Ponies*. New York, NY: Skyhorse Publishing, 2009.

Web Sites:

The Guide Horse Foundation
www.guidehorse.com/faq_horses.htm
Read about and see photos of miniature guide horses.

The Miniature Horse.com
www.theminiaturehorse.com
Follow this site's links to read about the history of miniature horses, their care, and their uses.

Index

baby 4, 6

barn 10

breed 4, 7

circuses 8

clubs 18

coat 16, 17

Dervish 20

eat 13

Einstein 21

England 9

farrier 14

grains 13

grass 13

Great Britain 8

groom 17

guide horses 20

hair 16, 17

hay 13

hoofs 14, 18

mare 19

mines 8

obey 18

pasture 10, 13

pets 8, 17, 18

pony 4, 5

race 8

ride 9, 15

salt 13

shed 16

shots 14

shows 8, 18

stallion 19

sweets 13

teeth 14

Thumbelina 20, 21

United States 8, 9

veterinarian 14

water 13

work 8